Design David West
          Children's Book Design
Editorial Planning Clark Robinson Ltd
Editor Bibby Whittaker
Researcher Cecilia Weston-Baker
Illustrated by Peter Bull, Rob Shone
          and Aziz Khan

EDITORIAL PANEL

The author, Robin Kerrod, is an
award-winning writer who
specializes in books on science.

The educational consultant, Peter
Thwaites, is Headmaster of
Northaw School, Salisbury,
Wiltshire, England.

The editorial consultant, John
Clark, has contributed to many
information and reference books.

*First published in
the United States in 1990 by*
Gloucester Press
387 Park Avenue South
New York NY 10016

ISBN 0 531 17222 8

Library of Congress Catalog
Card No: 89 81608

Printed in Belgium

TODAY'S WORLD

THE REVOLUTION IN INDUSTRY

ROBIN KERROD

GLOUCESTER PRESS
New York · London · Toronto · Sydney

CONTENTS

This diagram shows a modern steel-making plant, from receipt of iron ore by boat, to the making of steel, and the processing of steel ingots into flat sheets.

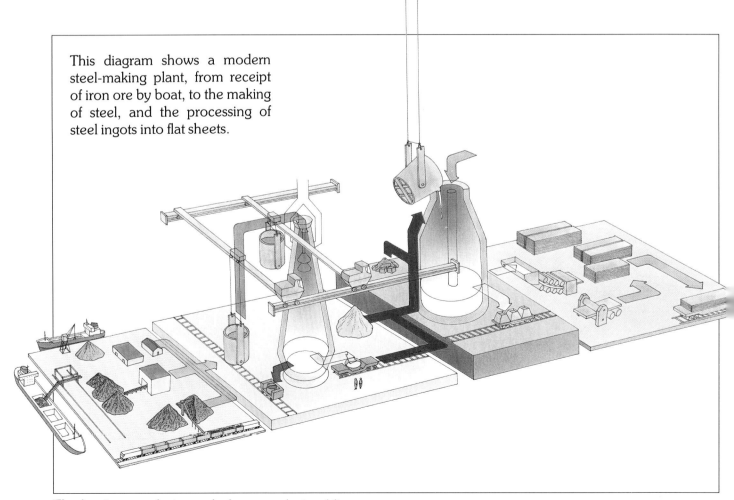

The front cover photograph shows a robot welding.

INTRODUCTION

What people can make has always influenced how people live. Nobody knows who first chipped a lump of flint and made a sharp cutting edge, but in doing so, he or she gave rise to the Stone Age, which lasted for two million years.

Modern man has been around for about 50,000 years. In 10,000 B.C. the population of the world was about ten million. People of that time lived by hunting animals and gathering food where they could find it. The rise of civilization depended on farming and a settled way of life, and farming developed very slowly. The first Industrial Revolution, which began about 200 years ago, started with the invention of farm machinery that could do the work formerly done by laborers and animals.

Today, with a world population approaching six billion, the most valuable commodity, after food, is information. The latest industrial revolution stems from new ways of dealing with information — gathering, storing, processing and transmitting it, usually with computers. The speed with which information is now passed has enabled huge advances to take place in industry. And this evolution has happened in a tiny space of time, compared to the immense span of history.

Dozens of electronics factories in Silicon Valley, California

INDUSTRIAL REVOLUTIONS

The world's first iron bridge spans the River Severn at Coalbrookdale, England. It was built in 3 months in 1779, using 378.5 tons of iron. Engines are rated in horsepower because in 1782 when a steam engine replaced 12 horses used at one mill, it was rated at "12 horsepower."

In the beginning, the Industrial Revolution was about hot, smoky furnaces which smelted iron or fired pottery. Iron was made into great steam engines that pumped coal mines dry, or powered mills where cloth was woven. Many things, such as tools and clothing were sold for the first time at prices people could afford. In the 18th century, canals and tunnels were dug and roads and bridges built. People and goods could now travel much more easily. In the 19th century, new discoveries were made and great wealth created. Now there is a new industrial revolution all about computers. It is very different from the first Industrial Revolution. The availability of labor is no longer a worry, but there are now limited resources of energy and materials.

17th Century

The stagecoach of the 17th century had a long history behind it. There were carts with wheels in 3000 B.C. But the earliest wheels were simply round shapes cut from trees. The spoked wheels of the stagecoach were light and strong. They were built by skilled craftsmen called wheelwrights. The coach itself was carefully, even luxuriously, designed. It carried passengers and their luggage over rough roads. Such coaches ran regularly between towns and cities and provided a service like a modern bus.

1881

When this practical, lightweight steam car of 1881 was first driven, inventors had been experimenting with steam-powered vehicles for more than 100 years. At the turn of the century, steam-driven road vehicles were faster than gasoline-engined cars. But they had to carry a heavy load of fuel to heat the water in the boiler. The water was used up very quickly. Steam cars had to stop after only a few miles to refill with water, and also to refuel. The design of gasoline driven cars improved rapidly, and soon they could go farther and faster.

CAD (Computer-Aided Design) helps engineers design a product, such as a new car headlight. First it is drawn on a computer monitor. The computer program can calculate how much material is needed to make the part or how aerodynamic it is. Advanced forms of CAD can also instruct machines in the factory how to make the new headlight and also how to test it.

Today

In a modern car factory, robots do two out of three of the jobs that used to be done by car workers. They install the doors, windows, and engines and weld the roof in place. The cars move past groups of robots on a production line. The cars are also painted and tested by robots. Each stage of manufacture is controlled by a computer. The computer is programed to make the right number of each model of car, order ready-made parts to the assembly line, and report errors. Such a factory works 24 hours a day, every day.

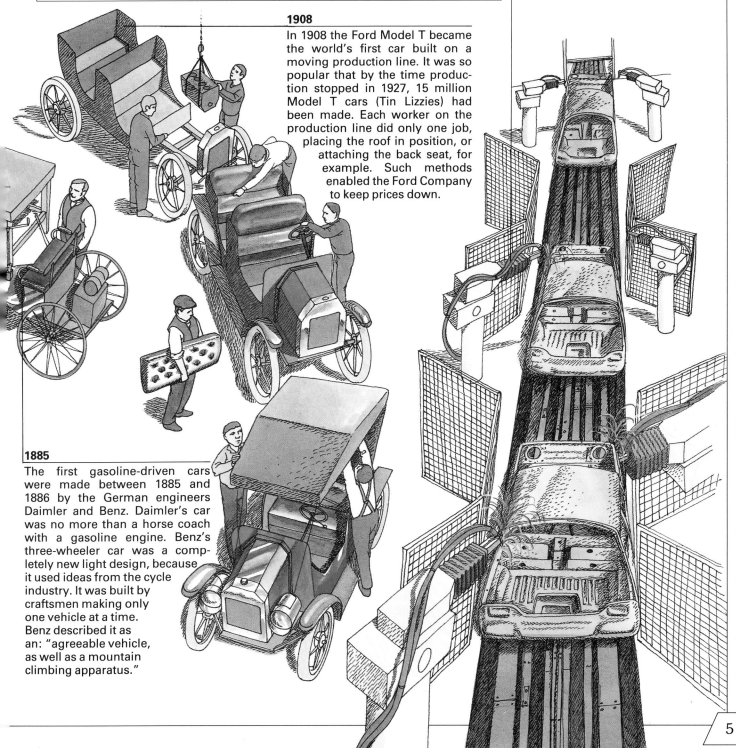

1908

In 1908 the Ford Model T became the world's first car built on a moving production line. It was so popular that by the time production stopped in 1927, 15 million Model T cars (Tin Lizzies) had been made. Each worker on the production line did only one job, placing the roof in position, or attaching the back seat, for example. Such methods enabled the Ford Company to keep prices down.

1885

The first gasoline-driven cars were made between 1885 and 1886 by the German engineers Daimler and Benz. Daimler's car was no more than a horse coach with a gasoline engine. Benz's three-wheeler car was a completely new light design, because it used ideas from the cycle industry. It was built by craftsmen making only one vehicle at a time. Benz described it as an: "agreeable vehicle, as well as a mountain climbing apparatus."

CHIPS AND ROBOTS

At the General Motors Corporation factory at Orion Township, U.S.A., more than one thousand computers are programed to control the entire factory.

The word "robot" was first used by the Czech playwright, Carel Capek, in his play "Rossum's Universal Robots."

Microprocessors (silicon chips) were invented in 1971. Already the value of industries making and using chips is greater than the value of the world's steel industry. The tiny chip, only 10 millimeters square, is packed with hundreds of thousands of transistors. They are at the heart of all computers and calculators. They can do a wide variety of jobs. Microprocessors control radiotelescopes and robots, jumbo jets and satellites, washing machines and electronic toys. And they made possible today's information-based industrial revolution.

Microtechnology

In 1948 the transistor was invented at Bell Telephone Laboratories. This minute device needs very little electricity and is supremely reliable. Early electronic computers used thousands of vacuum tubes and were huge. They broke down often. The computer based on the transistor changed all this. Soon thousands of transistors could be made, using a chemical etching process, on a single chip. Such microtechnology is used to make silicon chips for today's computers, specialist chips for fax machines, typesetting machines, CD players and television sets. One product of microtechnology is the very accurate quartz watch.

An automatic typesetting machine

Robots

There are now thousands of robots at work in factories around the world. These robots resemble giant mechanical arms. They perform the same very precise movements over and over again without mistake, using gears and rotating joints (see diagram, below). The first industrial robots could carry out only one simple task. A modern computer controlled robot can easily be programed, for example, to paint refrigerators one day, and electric fans the next day. Special kinds of robot can operate in a nuclear plant where it is unsafe for humans to go.

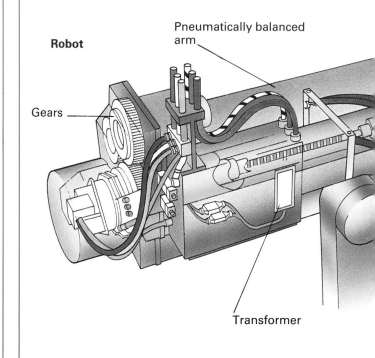

Robot

Pneumatically balanced arm

Gears

Transformer

Precise control

The precisely controlled light emitted by lasers is used for both high-speed and color printing. Surveyors now beam laser light to measure the height of distant mountains. Minute lasers track recorded sound on compact discs (CDs). In medicine they can replace the surgeon's knife. Powerful industrial lasers cut and drill the hardest metals. Small lasers read the barcodes on products at supermarket checkouts. Color laser lights make patterns in spectacular light shows. Lasers are found wherever exact measurement, or the application of power, is needed.

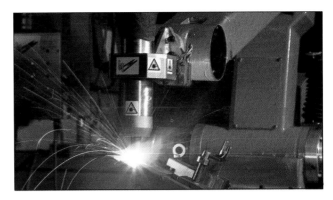

A robot arm laser welding two pieces of metal

Robot playing an electronic organ

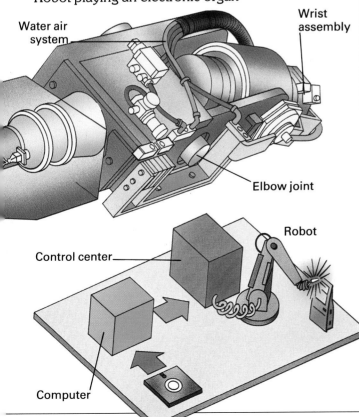

Water air system

Wrist assembly

Elbow joint

Robot

Control center

Computer

Automation

All aspects of human life are affected by automation – in an office where the payroll is prepared by computer; in banking where money is transferred electronically, and cash provided on demand by machine; airline reservations; electronic mail sorting – the list is endless. In automated factories, where complex goods such as washing machines or cars are constructed by robots, many intricate operations can take place without human intervention. In the chemical industry whole processes to make plastics, fertilizers or paints are precisely adjusted and controlled by automated machinery. Such machinery is always under constant human supervision and control.

A large automated printing press

Nylon was invented in 1935: 64 million pairs of nylon stockings were sold in 1939. By the 1970s, the American chemical industry dominated in the production of plastics. It made three million tons of polythene, 1.7 million tons of polystyrene and 1.3 million tons of PVC a year.

Our daily life has always been shaped by the materials we use. Most of our clothes, and the textiles, curtains and carpets in our homes, are man-made. Different man-made plastics are used to insulate and also to make electrical products such as telephones and televisions. In the Stone Age, people used the stones they found as tools and weapons. Later discoveries and techniques gave the Bronze Age and the Iron Age their names. Now we make far too many new materials to name periods of time after them. Some of these materials are described in this chapter.

Tailor-made

Tailor-made materials are materials designed for a specific use. Ordinary glass can shatter dangerously. But two layers of glass bonded together with a resin make safe, shatterproof laminated glass for car windshields. This is a tailor-made material. Plastics are another type of material that can be made to order, tailor-made by chemists. Plastics can be hard, soft, easily bent or stretched, or very stiff. They can be excellent electrical insulators, or can conduct electricity. Plastics can be made into thin, transparent films of any color. Some, like Teflon (PTFE), resist heat and are very slippery. Others, such as Kevlar, are stronger than steel. Most are made of petrochemicals.

Bronze, an alloy of copper and tin, was used 5,500 years ago in the Bronze Age. Now it is used in machines and at sea because it resists corrosion. Iron has been known for nearly as long but the Iron Age began only when a reliable method of working it was discovered 3,500 years ago. Really large-scale production of iron started the Industrial Revolution. In the 19th century, tough alloys of iron, called steel, were discovered. Steel manufacture is now one of the largest industries in the world. Stainless steel resists corrosion. Other steels are used in shipbuilding and skyscraper frames. Alloys of titanium are used in armaments and in the aerospace industry.

Tank armor is a metal/plastic composite.

Teflon lining a pan forms a non-stick coating.

Carbon fiber

Carbon fiber is made by heating rayon or pitch in an airless atmosphere. Carbon fibers do not melt or burn; they resist strong acids and alkalis and cannot be dissolved in any known solvent. They are used in the aerospace industry. Every modern jumbo jet (Boeing 747) contains about 2% CFRP (carbon fiber reinforced plastic). Carbon fibers make strong, light materials that conduct electricity. They are used for electrical connections in the pacemakers that control weak hearts. In sports, carbon fiber fishing rods and golf clubs are already in use.

Helicopter blades made from carbon fiber

Glass fiber

Many materials not thought of as very strong become so in the form of fibers. Glass is one of them. A fiber of glass is 100 times stronger than plain glass. Glass fiber has many uses: as an insulator, in car tires and in fireproof cloth. But one of its widespread uses is in glass reinforced plastic (GRP). This new material is ideal for maintenance-free boat hulls, car bodies, asbestos-free roofing panels, corrosion-proof pipes and in missile cases. Glass fibers are also the basis of fiber-optic cables, used for carrying telephone and television signals.

Telephone circuits linked to fiber-optic cables

Improving materials

One kind of ceramic – pottery – has been in use since the late Stone Age. It has provided a historical record of civilization around the world. This is because clay, the raw material used to make pots, is found nearly everywhere, and pieces of pot are nearly indestructable. Today glass, another ceramic, accounts for 45% of all ceramics made. New improved ceramics now replace metal parts of diesel engines. Such ceramics start from exotic chemical substances. These mixtures are heated in special furnaces by lasers or radio frequences to produce specialist materials required in the defense and space industries. Such materials protect space vehicles on re-entry into the Earth's atmosphere. Another type of ceramic may one day be used to make fuel cells which use a chemical process to convert fuels directly into electricity.

Workers stick ceramic tiles on the Space Shuttle.

METALS FOR INDUSTRY

8 percent of the Earth's crust consists of aluminum. There is more aluminum than any other metal in the world. It is found in all rocks except limestone and sandstone. Rubies and sapphires contain aluminum. An aluminum-air battery could provide pollution-free power.

The largest piece of copper ever found weighed about 400 tons. It was found in Minnesota in 1857. The largest nugget of native gold weighed 248 pounds.

A world without metals is difficult to imagine. Machines we now take for granted depend on a knowledge of the science and technology of metals. The core of a nuclear reactor is strong, resists great temperatures, and does not leak. To achieve such reliability, new alloys of iron and titanium have been invented, along with new methods of welding them together. New ways of testing metals using X rays and radioisotopes have been perfected. We depend now on the light alloys of aluminum for our aircraft, automobiles and spacecraft. Copper and its alloys, brass and bronze, are important in the electrical industry. Research shows that metals grown as single crystals are very strong because they are flawless. In future, civil engineering projects, such as bridges and tall buildings, will be designed with delicate, immensely strong structures of the new metals.

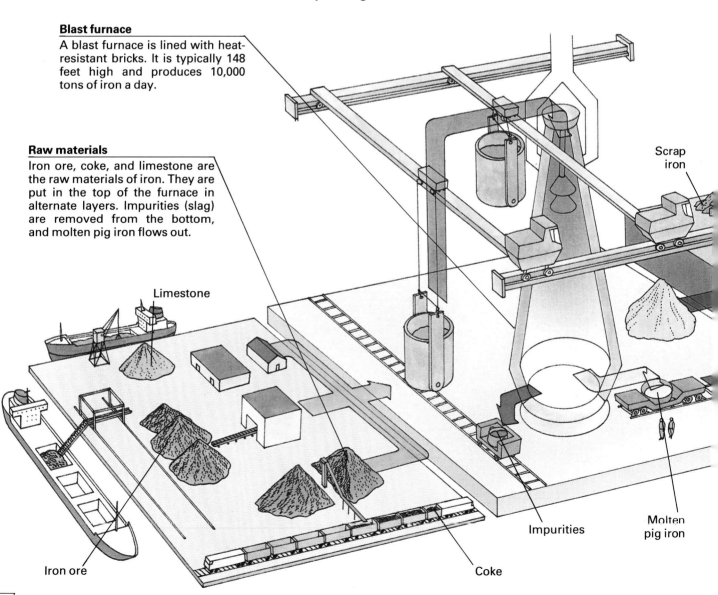

Blast furnace
A blast furnace is lined with heat-resistant bricks. It is typically 148 feet high and produces 10,000 tons of iron a day.

Raw materials
Iron ore, coke, and limestone are the raw materials of iron. They are put in the top of the furnace in alternate layers. Impurities (slag) are removed from the bottom, and molten pig iron flows out.

Limestone

Scrap iron

Iron ore

Coke

Impurities

Molten pig iron

Aluminum

Aluminum is made from its ore, alumina, in an electrolytic cell. The cell consists of a large steel box, lined with carbon. Alumina is melted, dissolved in another molten aluminum ore called cryolite. Electricity supplied to the cell causes pure aluminum to collect at the bottom of the cell, where it is siphoned off. The process requires enormous amounts of electricity. Today, nearly one-fifth of all aluminum is recycled.

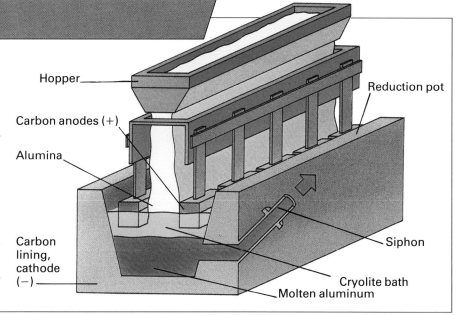

Hopper

Reduction pot

Carbon anodes (+)

Alumina

Carbon lining, cathode (−)

Siphon

Cryolite bath

Molten aluminum

Oxygen

Lime

Water-cooled lance

Oxygen process

In the oxygen process for making steel, almost pure oxygen is blown through a water-cooled lance onto the surface of the molten iron. The oxygen combines with the carbon in the molten metal to produce steel.

The furnace can take about 300 tons of iron, a third of which can be scrap iron. The furnace is tilted to pour out the molten steel in a shower of sparks. The steel is cast into ingots, ready for shaping by forging or rolling.

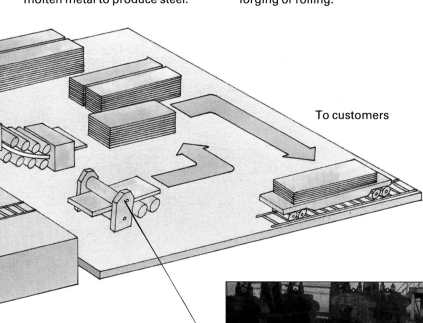

To customers

Steel ingots

A steel-making complex

At one end of the steel mill, the raw materials are delivered. These are made into iron in giant blast furnaces. The pig iron produced is converted into steel in a second furnace. The steel is then shaped, usually by rolling.

Shaping

Most steel products are made from steel that has first been cast into ingots. Hot ingots are rolled into the required shape. Other steel products are hammered or forged into shape. Some steels, such as wires, are extruded forced through a small hole.

A rolling mill at a steelworks

In 1981 the supertanker *Seawise Giant* was built. Its length was 1,600 feet, and it was the first ship to exceed half a million tons deadweight. It is unlikely such a large supertanker will be built again, because it cannot pass through the Panama or Suez Canals.

New ways to design, build and use ships are constantly being discovered. As soon as more passengers crossed the Atlantic by plane than by ship, large liners became luxury cruise ships. Today's giants of the oceans are vast oil and gas tankers, bulk cargo vessels and superfast container ships. Roll on, roll off (RORO) ferries carry cars, passengers and trucks. In the future there will probably be nuclear-powered ships, or sail-assisted cargo vessels, navigating by satellite and controlled by computer, and these will be produced in modern specialized shipbuilding yards.

Modular construction

Traditionally, the building of a large ship started by laying the keel. Then the ribs were added to give shape to the hull. The hull was completed by riveting or welding metal plates to the ribs. The rest of the ship could then be built. New methods of construction were developed as ships, especially oil tankers, grew larger. In modular construction, different sections of the ship (bow, middle, stern) are completed separately. The sections are brought together and joined to make a ship of the required length. Some small vessels are made this way now, since each section can be completed indoors.

Newly-built ships being fitted out

Building ships in modules

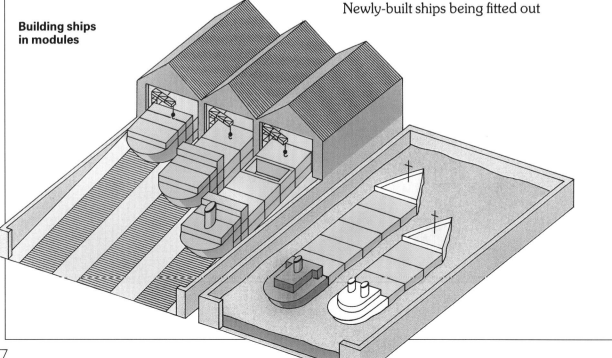

Welding and riveting

Welding is the main method of construction used in shipbuilding. In welding, a flame melts the edges of the metal parts to be joined. The metal then flows together and hardens when the heat is removed. More metal can be added to strengthen the join.

To weld steel, oxygen and acetylene gases, under pressure, are fed into the welding torch. Oxygen and hydrogen gases are necessary to weld stainless steel or aluminum. An electric arc provides the heat in another method of welding.

Where weight is less important, riveting can be used. Here, a red-hot piece of metal called a rivet, shaped like a bolt, is passed through holes in both pieces of metal. The headless end of the rivet is hammered until the pieces are held firmly together.

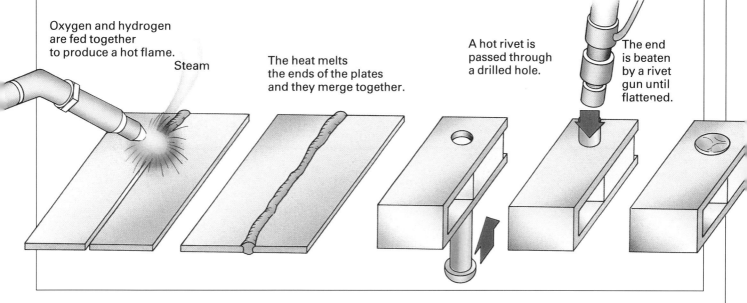

Oxygen and hydrogen are fed together to produce a hot flame.

Steam

The heat melts the ends of the plates and they merge together.

A hot rivet is passed through a drilled hole.

The end is beaten by a rivet gun until flattened.

Propellers

The first steam ships used paddle wheels. In rough seas, paddle wheels lift out of the water. Because people were not convinced that propellers could do the job of paddle wheels, the British Royal Navy arranged a test in 1845 to see which was better. Two frigates, the propeller-driven *Rattler* and the *Alecto*, equipped with paddle wheels, were used. First the *Rattler* won a 93 mile race by several miles. Next, the *Alecto*, linked to the *Rattler* by a hawser, was pulled backward at a rate of three knots. The sceptics were convinced.

The world's largest propeller was made in 1982 for a 208,000-ton bulk-ore tanker *Hoei Maru*. This propeller was 36 feet in diameter. Submarines have silent propellers to escape detection by an enemy, and ferries have sideways propellers to maneuver in harbors without the help of tugboats. Some new types of ship such as hovercraft or hydrofoils have airplane propellers.

A huge propeller is carefully balanced.

The Boeing 747 "jumbo jet" flies at 621 miles per hour and is 230 feet long. This is a greater distance than the first powered flight (131 feet) by Orville Wright. The jumbo weighs more than 77,093 pounds and can fly for a distance of more than 10,313 miles non-stop.

No single invention apart from the wheel has changed transportation as much as the airplane. High speed travel everywhere has made the world seem smaller. Mass tourism to familiar and to exotic places has changed the way people live and how they enjoy their leisure. Aircraft have affected the way war is waged. Goods that used to travel by ship now arrive much sooner by aircraft. The aerospace industry has encouraged the invention and use of new materials. These include metal alloys and specially tailored synthetic materials based on ceramics and carbon fiber.

Construction

Fuselage assembly

Wings fitted

Tail structure added

Large jet aircraft are made in giant factories that occupy as much space as a major shipyard. Many aircraft are assembled at the same time and they are all in different stages of completion. Each aircraft may be intended for a different customer. Completed wings, fuselage parts and engines are brought together and fitted by skilled workers. Riveted aluminum structures are increasingly being replaced by CFRPs (carbon fiber reinforced plastics), which bond the lightweight aluminum around tubular frames (see inset). The control system and engines are installed and carefully tested, and like many parts the engines are supplied by specialist companies. Finally, when everything has been checked on the ground, the aircraft is taken for a test flight.

Making a section of fuselage

International cooperation

The Airbus A300B first flew in 1972. This airliner is one of the best in the world. The wings are built in Britain, and the slats and flaps in the Netherlands. Sections of fuselage are made in West Germany, and the nose in France. The tailplane and doors are Spanish, and the two mighty engines are constructed in the United States. Although this aircraft has only two engines, it has the best safety record of any now flying. Military aircraft, such as the *Jaguar*, have also been built cooperatively.

The only airliner to fly faster than the speed of sound in regular service is the *Concorde*. This extraordinary aircraft was planned in the 1950s, and construction began in 1962. Only 16 *Concordes* were built as part of a cooperative project between Britain and France. Powered by British Olympus jet engines, the *Concorde* flies between Britain and the United States in just over 3 hours.

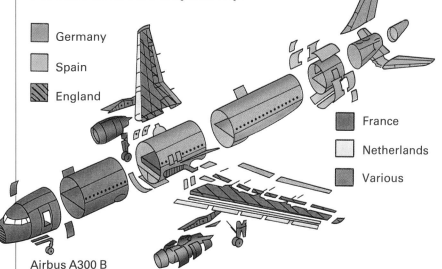

■ Germany
■ Spain
▨ England

■ France
□ Netherlands
■ Various

Airbus A300 B

Final assembly of the *Concorde*

Control system fitted

Engines installed

Turbine blades

When the fuel in a jet engine burns, it produces very high temperatures. These temperatures (higher than 3,632°F) mean that no ordinary metal can be used to make the turbine blades. Instead, special heat resistant alloys of the metals titanium, vanadium and molybdenum have been developed to make them.

Turbine blades for a turbofan engine

CHEMICAL INDUSTRY

One of the first attempts to make synthetic ivory resulted in explosive billiard balls.

About 17,000 different chemical smells have been described. The worst smell of all is that of the chemical ethyl mercaptan – which smells like a mixture of rotting cabbage, sewer gas and garlic.

Chemists have discovered 7 million different chemical substances, and many thousands more are found each year.

Today's chemical industry, based firmly on science, grew enormously in this century. It started with the manufacture of the alkalis soda and caustic soda, by processes discovered in the 19th century. These processes led to new ways of making sulfuric acid, ammonia and, from ammonia, nitric acid. Powerful explosives such as dynamite and the discovery of synthetic dyes opened the way to the modern chemical industry. Typical products are fertilizers and, above all, petrochemicals – this includes plastics, man-made fibers and raw materials for other industries. The first chemical in general use was common salt. This is usually mined from underground deposits which are remains of dried-up seas. Modern chemistry now links with biochemistry and the science of medicine to produce a wide variety of drugs.

Chemical plant for the manufacture of sulfuric acid

Oil industry

Countless chemicals called petrochemicals are made from oil in millions of tons each year. This is in addition to the use of oil as a fuel and a lubricant. Oil is a fossil fuel, generally found underground. Crude oil is virtually useless, and it has to be refined. The refined oil is heated, and different fractions boil off and are collected. Each of these has a particular use. Also heavy oils can be made into more useful fuels by heating them strongly with a catalyst (a chemical that makes a reaction take place faster, without being changed itself). This breaks the long heavy oil molecules into shorter volatile molecules, a process called cracking.

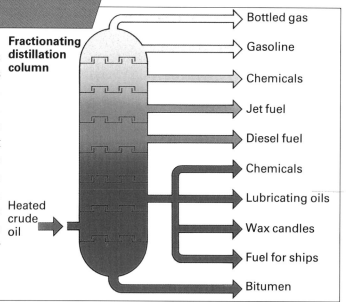

Fractionating distillation column

Heated crude oil

- Bottled gas
- Gasoline
- Chemicals
- Jet fuel
- Diesel fuel
- Chemicals
- Lubricating oils
- Wax candles
- Fuel for ships
- Bitumen

Making sulfuric acid: (1) sulfur is burned to produce sulfur dioxide gas. (2) Electrostatic removal of dust. (3) The gas is cooled, (4) scrubbed clean and (5) washed. (6) Sulfur dioxide is mixed with oxygen (vanadium oxide catalyst), to make Sulfur trioxide. (7) This gas is cooled, and (8) is absorbed, leaving sulfuric acid to run off.

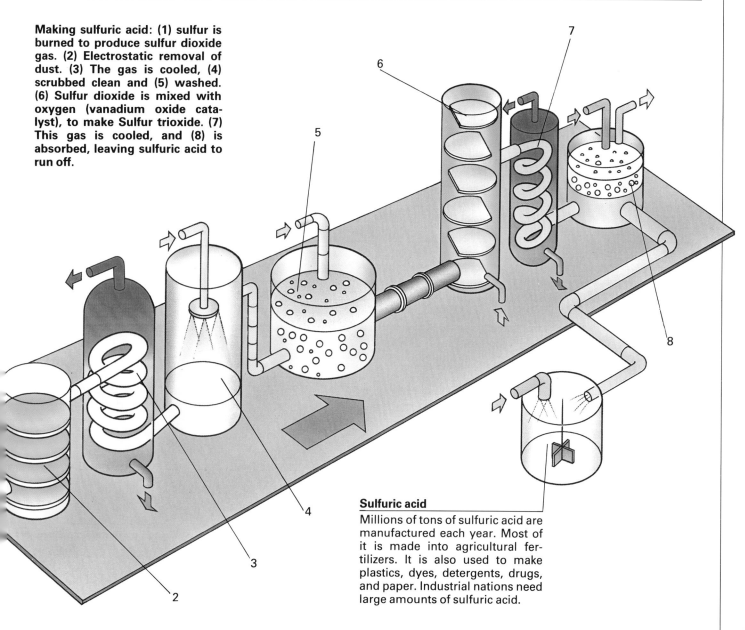

Sulfuric acid

Millions of tons of sulfuric acid are manufactured each year. Most of it is made into agricultural fertilizers. It is also used to make plastics, dyes, detergents, drugs, and paper. Industrial nations need large amounts of sulfuric acid.

Variety of textures

The chemical industry makes the plastics we see all around us: bowls, mops and buckets. Electrical devices such as telephones, televisions, and microwave ovens make use of plastic. In the car, there are many plastic materials. A chemist calls the molecules in plastic polymers. Polymers are long molecules that are different in each plastic. Different polymers make the plastic strong, soft, stiff or bendable. Nylon is a very strong polymer, and has many uses as a solid or a fiber.

A hair comb made from nylon

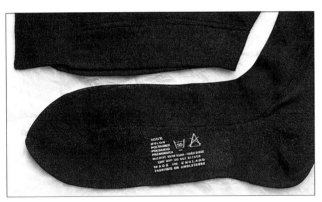

Socks woven from nylon fiber

Nylon gears inside a chain saw

Detergent and soap

Soap was first made more than 5,000 years ago. During most of this time it was made by boiling animal fat with ashes (ashes are alkalis). Modern soap manufacture uses caustic soda (a strong alkali) and fats and vegetable oils. Oils and fats are boiled with alkali at a very high temperature. The resulting solid soap is cleaned, perfumed and pressed into shape for sale.

Synthetic soaps are called detergents. Detergents are petrochemicals because they are made from byproducts of petroleum.

Soaps and detergents clean clothes in the same way, because their molecules are alike. One end of the molecule buries itself in a greasy dirt particle. The other end stays in the water and removes the dirt particle by making it dissolve in water. Household detergents may contain bleaches, brighteners and perfumes. Modern detergents are biodegradable; they break down when washed away so that they do not remain in streams and rivers and cause pollution.

A boat spraying detergent on an oil slick

Textiles

Textiles are any fabrics. They can be made from either natural fibers such as wool and cotton, or from synthetic fibers. Rayon, the first successful synthetic fiber, is made by chemically treating cellulose, a typical product of wood. It was without a rival until nylon was invented.

Most modern fibers that are used to make textiles are petrochemicals. Each fiber consists of long chains of molecules. Chemists change these molecules at will to make the woven textiles strong for sails, soft for knitted sweaters or hard as steel for bullet-proof vests.

Textiles have always been dyed. The colors used were from vegetables and animals. Chemical dyestuffs designed to color textiles made from natural fibers do not work well on man-made fibers. So new dyestuffs have been invented to provide bright colors that do not fade.

Modern textiles of all colors

A close-up of the loops and hooks of a Velcro fastening

Drugs

Drugs are obtained from various sources. Some antibiotics are made from molds, other drugs are extracted from plants, but most are produced from petrochemicals. Antibiotics and sulfonamides have saved millions of lives. These drugs kill the bacteria that cause disease. Infections that were fatal not long ago are now cured daily by a few pills. Drugs called beta-blockers are used successfully to treat high blood pressure. These are sometimes used together with other drugs called diuretics. Pharmaceutical companies search for new drugs, particularly alkaloids, in plants, as well as seeking to improve existing remedies.

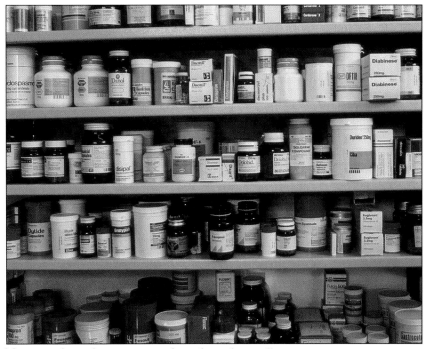

Most modern drugs are produced synthetically.

DOMESTIC APPLIANCES

The vacuum cleaner was invented in 1901. Early models were as large as a small car, and operated by three men.

The first electric refrigerator went on sale in Chicago in 1927. Microwave ovens, using the same principle as radar, first appeared in 1947.

New possessions in the home that affect how we live and entertain ourselves include the freezer and the microwave oven. Most people have washing machines, many have tumble driers and dishwashers. Nearly everyone has a color television set and either a tape recorder or a video cassette recorder. Important changes in the home also took place during the 18th and 19th centuries. These also affected how everyone lived. One was the invention of modern sanitation. Another change was the switch from oil lighting to gas lighting and later to electricity.

Parts from everywhere

Supplying the modern home with everything from cutlery to video cassette recorders involves many different industries throughout the world. Your knives, spoons and forks may be made from Korean stainless steel; your curtains from fabrics woven in India. Wooden furniture may be made in the town where you live from timber imported from South America or the Philippines.

Modern manufacturing can be an extremely complicated process. To be able to sell a washing machine at a competitive price, its maker will have to buy materials and parts from many countries. The company that makes the stainless steel drum may not be able to supply the mild steel panels for the case. A specialist manufacturer supplies the insulating plastics that make the machine operate efficiently; another provides the electronics that control the washing cycles. The hoses and seals are made by another company. There must be standardization for this system to work: it helps if everyone uses the metric system, for example. And it is important that manufacturers in different countries use the same standards for electrical safety. The role of the parent manufacturing company now becomes that of an assembler of parts in the most economical way.

Robot assembling components

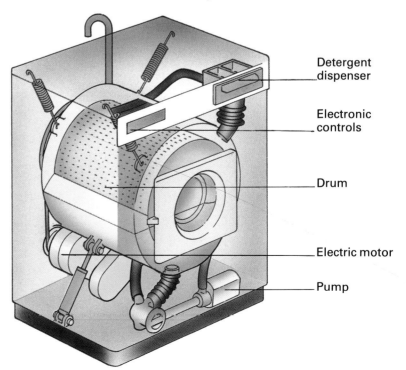

Detergent dispenser

Electronic controls

Drum

Electric motor

Pump

New materials

Some new materials in the home are not as new as they appear to be. Veneering, in which a thin layer of an expensive and decorative wood is glued to a plain and cheap wood, is an old craft. This process has now reappeared and been adapted in the manufacture of plastic laminates. The top layer of the laminate is made to resemble wood or tiles, or simply a colorful pattern.

The laminate is glued to chipboard, a synthetic wood made by embedding wood waste in a resin, to make kitchen cabinets. Chipboard is also used for floorboards. Floors are covered with durable vinyl tiles or carpets woven from synthetic fiber. An appliance such as a microwave oven uses many materials and components: metals, plastics, glass and electronic circuits.

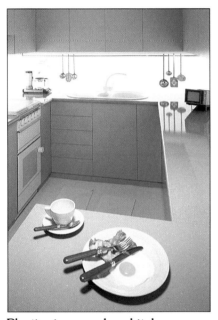

Plastics in a modern kitchen

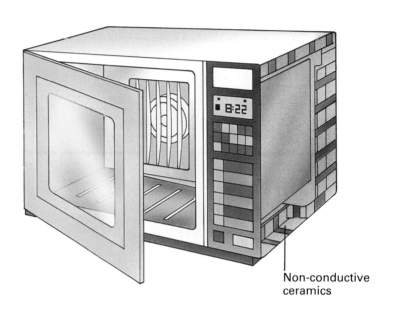

Non-conductive ceramics

Mixtures of materials

There is a very wide choice of new and different materials. This enables the designer of, for example, a new vacuum cleaner to be highly selective. Just the right combination of light and strong metals and plastics can be specified in the design. Because each material is selected for its ability to do the job, the appliance is very reliable. It makes economical use of resources: a modern washing machine uses less water and electricity than one designed only a few years ago. It is also quieter, because it is insulated for sound as well as for loss of heat.

Efficient vacuum cleaners are widely and cheaply available because they make good use of mixtures of new materials. Even the bright colors we take for granted all around us depend on new paint technology.

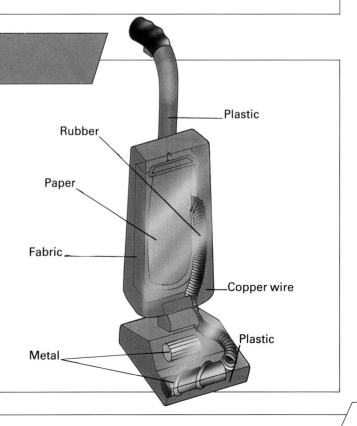

Plastic

Rubber

Paper

Fabric

Copper wire

Plastic

Metal

Boring an underground railroad tunnel

Elevated sections

Elevated sections of a highway can be built as part of a complex interchange where the driver can leave one highway and join another without impeding the flow of traffic.

Reshaping the landscape

Here an old country road is to be replaced by a highway. 1. The ground for the new road is bulldozed, leveled and prepared for its concrete surface. 2. An overpass is constructed to give access to a new factory. 3. When the work is completed, the quarry is landscaped and replanted with trees.

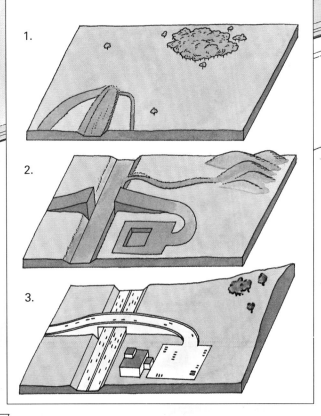

1.

2.

3.

Cranes

Powerful tower derricks are seen on building sites of all kinds. the pivoted end of the jib may move up and down the construction as needed.

First concrete

Ready-mixed concrete is fed into a paver, which creeps along depositing an even layer of concrete. The first layer is compacted using machines called vibrators.

The concrete "train" automates the process of making a road. The road is laid as a continuous slab of concrete. The slab is 33 feet wide. The train consumes 300 tons of material every hour. The base of the road consists of a layer of stones or gravel. A concrete road spreads the load of heavy vehicles.

The Great Wall of China is estimated to be 1,696 miles long (the distance from London to Athens). It is the only man-made object visible from space.

The Romans used a kind of concrete, called pozzolana, (mixed lime and volcanic ash).

The largest concrete structure in the world is the Grand Coulee Dam on the Columbia River, in the state of Washington.

What we now call civil engineering – the construction of roads, bridges, and canals – has had a very long history. At first, there were only empirical methods of construction: there was no underlying theory or calculation based on accurate knowledge. Some of the first exact methods of calculation were discovered by military engineers, and the Romans were excellent road builders. Leonardo da Vinci conducted the first exact experiments on the strength of materials. Such experiments are now taken for granted. Today's civil engineer computes first and builds second. Whole buildings and even cities can be modelled by a computer, changed and redesigned at will.

Final layer
Steel reinforcing is laid over the first layer of still wet concrete. A second layer is put over the steel, leveled, and given a non-skid surface.

Tunneling
Tunnels can be made in several different ways. One way is to dig a trench, lay the tunnel, and fill in over it. Undersea tunnels can be made onshore and then laid on the seabed. A tunnel can also be dug out and shored up as it progresses.

BRIDGES AND TUNNELS

The longest tunnel in the world is 105 miles long. It is the New York City West Delaware water supply tunnel.

The longest railroad tunnel and double-deck bridge are Japanese. The Oshimizu tunnel is 13.8 mi and the Akashi-Kaikyo bridge is 1.1 miles long.

Big projects, such as a long bridge, deep tunnel or oil-platform construction, benefit from new knowledge of materials, and new, highly accurate measuring techniques. Special steels and anti-corrosion paints are used for bridges. The towers of the largest suspension bridges are constructed taking the curvature of the Earth into consideration. North Sea oil-drilling platforms are placed exactly in position using navigational satellites to ensure accuracy. Laser surveying techniques help engineers to bore tunnels at the correct depth and in exactly the right direction.

Bridges

Early bridges were probably simply logs or slabs of stone laid across streams. Later bridges used wooden tressles or steel trusses, or arches built of stone or brick; arch bridges are now made from reinforced concrete. Curiously, the suspended bridge, a type of construction used now to make the longest bridges of all, is also one of the most primitive. It was used by the Incas. They took jungle vines and split bamboo and spanned the deepest mountain ravines. Modern versions of such bridges are still made and are in daily use in developing countries; this contrasts with the massive new bridges that span the rivers and waterways of the Western World.

A rope and wood suspension bridge in Asia

Tunneling

Large-scale tunneling through soft rock or clay depends on a tunneling machine called the mole. This machine uses a huge, many-bladed circular knife under hydraulic control. As it rotates, it bores out the tunnel. At the same time the tunnel is lined with prefabricated concrete sections bolted together. These sections have to be watertight to prevent underground water seeping into the tunnel and flooding the work.

If the rock is too hard for the mole to bore through, explosives have to be used to blast the rock away. With either method, the rubble produced in tunneling is carried away by a conveyor belt to the tunnel entrance.

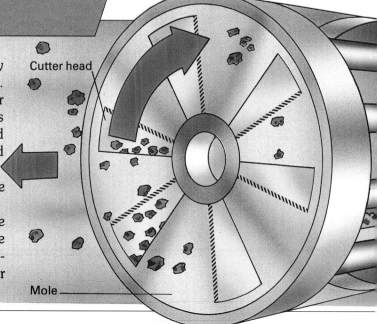

Cutter head

Mole

There are four main types of bridge: beam, arch, suspension and cantilever. Their construction depends on two basic manufacturing processes: the mass-production of quality steel, and cement for making concrete. Some bridges such as Tower Bridge, London, combine more than one type of construction (in this case beam and cantilever; a cantilever is a beam that is supported at one end). The towers of a suspension bridge are often keyed into bedrock, and the cables suspending the bridge are equally firmly anchored.

Hollow caissons form the foundations

Crane is used to construct towers

Wires are pulled across

Box sections are lifted into place

Sections are joined together

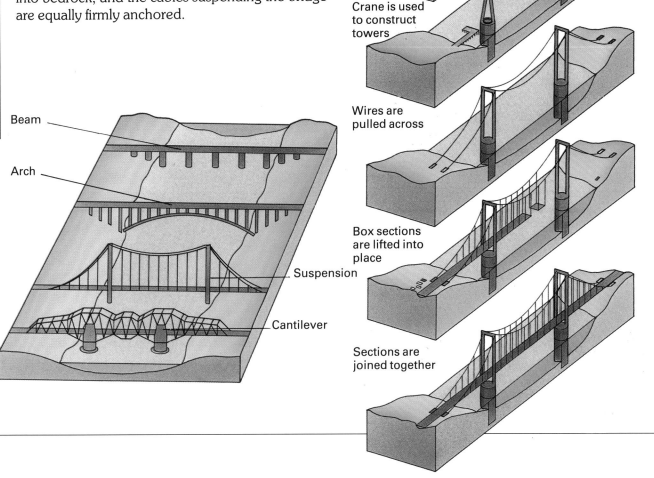

Beam

Arch

Suspension

Cantilever

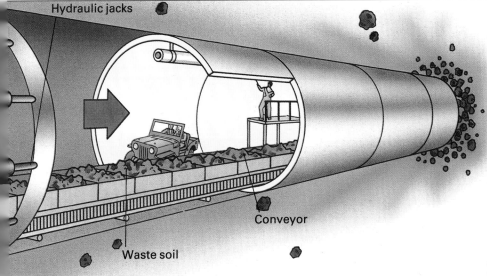

Hydraulic jacks

Conveyor

Waste soil

Building the Channel Tunnel

LARGE BUILDINGS

The world's tallest tower, the C.N. Tower in the Metro Centre, Toronto, Canada, is 1,821 feet high. It has a revolving restaurant 1,139 feet from the ground that seats 416 diners. The tower, made of reinforced concrete, weighs 130,000 tons. It is topped by a transmission mast.

Modern buildings, such as skyscrapers, are constructed using sophisticated and powerful equipment operated by comparatively few people. Today, the use of iron and steel in construction places no practical limit on the height of a building, and towers more than six-tenths of a mile tall have been planned. In contrast, the large buildings of the past were built with primitive equipment and vast numbers of workers. The height of buildings such as medieval cathedrals was also limited by the strength of the stone used.

Under one roof

There are many reasons for large buildings. One is to make the best use of expensive land in cities. Another is the efficient housing of all the staff of large companies together. Large buildings are like villages or small towns. There are services such as hairdressers, dry cleaners, pharmacists and restaurants. There is space for parking, swimming pools and squash courts in addition to the offices.

Other large buildings include warehouses, factories, sports arenas and aerospace assembly plants. These may not be tall, but they cover large areas. Special roof systems, such as domes made from many similar panels, are needed to span such a large space. Extra space, perhaps for an underground parking lot, is obtained by leaving room under the building itself.

A robot moving boxes in a warehouse

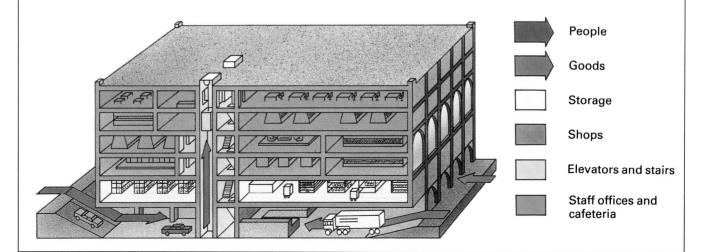

→ People

→ Goods

Storage

Shops

Elevators and stairs

Staff offices and cafeteria

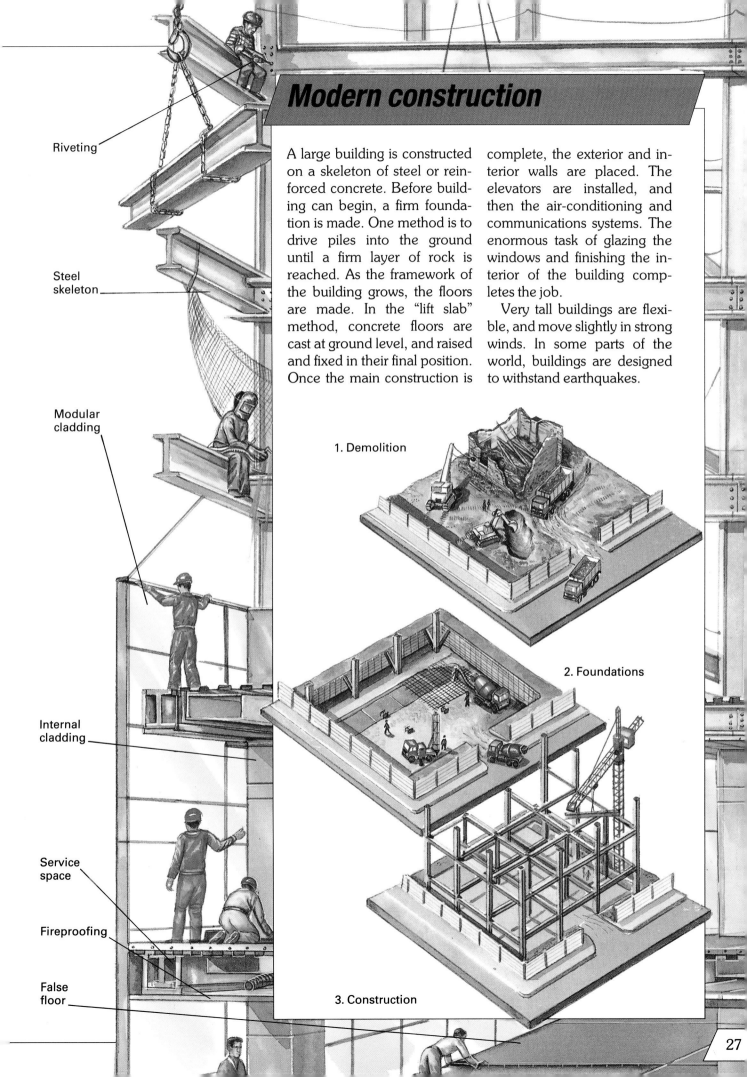

Modern construction

Riveting

Steel
skeleton

Modular
cladding

Internal
cladding

Service
space

Fireproofing

False
floor

A large building is constructed on a skeleton of steel or reinforced concrete. Before building can begin, a firm foundation is made. One method is to drive piles into the ground until a firm layer of rock is reached. As the framework of the building grows, the floors are made. In the "lift slab" method, concrete floors are cast at ground level, and raised and fixed in their final position. Once the main construction is complete, the exterior and interior walls are placed. The elevators are installed, and then the air-conditioning and communications systems. The enormous task of glazing the windows and finishing the interior of the building completes the job.

Very tall buildings are flexible, and move slightly in strong winds. In some parts of the world, buildings are designed to withstand earthquakes.

1. Demolition

2. Foundations

3. Construction

The world's tallest office building is the Sears Tower, in Chicago, Illinois. The population of the building is nearly 17,000 people, who are served by more than 100 elevators and nearly 20 escalators. The building has 16,000 windows, almost one per person, to be kept clean! This building tells us much about service industry. Nearly everyone now in it is employed by a service industry. The building itself was built by a traditional industry, construction.

Today in the United States, Japan and the rich, industrialized nations of Europe, more people are employed in service industries than in heavy industry, manufacturing, and agriculture. Service industries are businesses that support traditional industry. They include public transportation; the supply of electricity, gas and water; shops, hotels and security; and businesses connected with sports and leisure activities.

Manufacturing and service industries make increasing use of computers to help them run efficiently. As a result, people working in both manufacturing and service industries work fewer hours and have more leisure time.

Transportation

Fast, reliable transportation provides a vital service to industry. Factories no longer keep vast stocks of supplies such as spare parts or raw materials. Nor do they keep big stocks of finished products. Managers must be able to obtain new supplies quickly to meet customers' orders. When the products are made, they must be delivered promptly. People, too, depend on an efficient transportation system. The traveler by air, sea, road or rail makes use of a worldwide service industry, the travel industry.

A variety of service industries are needed to run a large office building in the business center of a modern city. A selection of some of them are shown and described on this and the following three pages.

Large trains carry freight by rail.

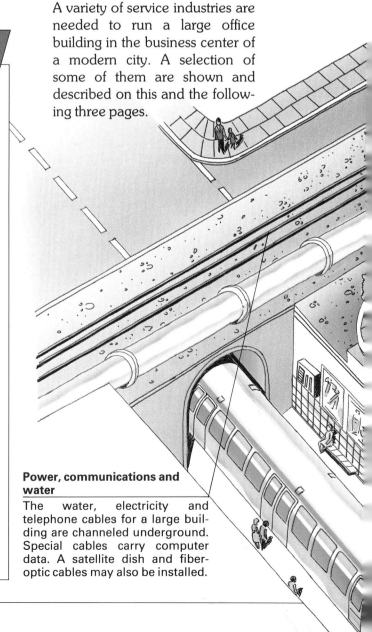

Power, communications and water

The water, electricity and telephone cables for a large building are channeled underground. Special cables carry computer data. A satellite dish and fiber-optic cables may also be installed.

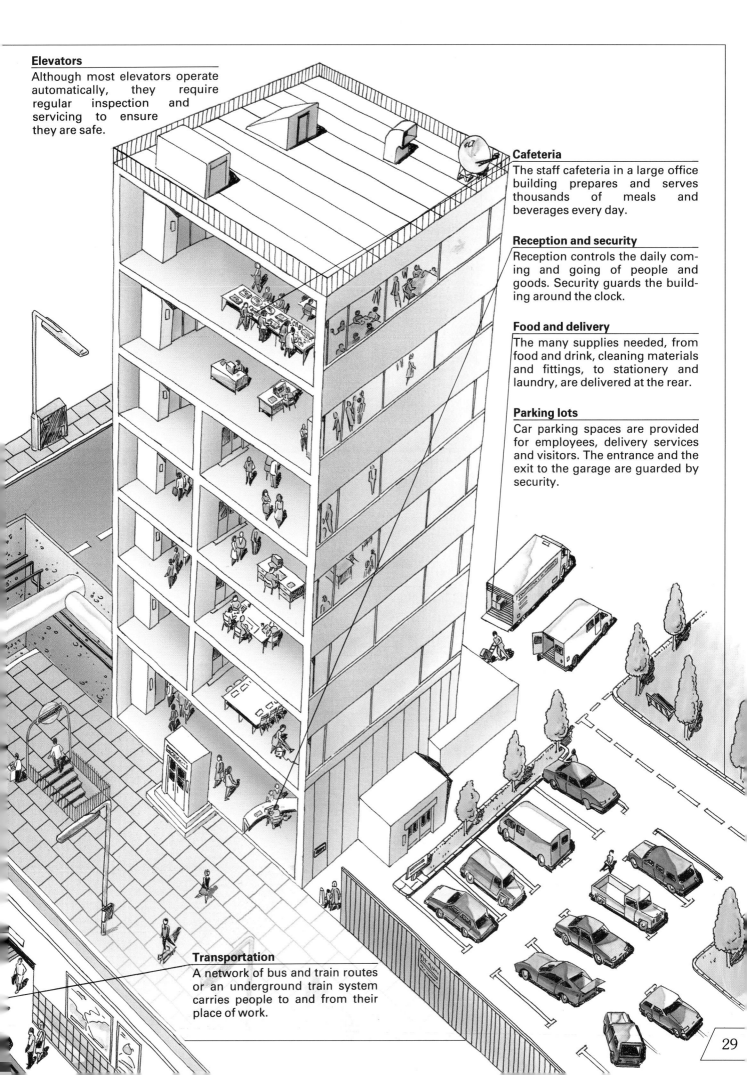

Elevators

Although most elevators operate automatically, they require regular inspection and servicing to ensure they are safe.

Cafeteria

The staff cafeteria in a large office building prepares and serves thousands of meals and beverages every day.

Reception and security

Reception controls the daily coming and going of people and goods. Security guards the building around the clock.

Food and delivery

The many supplies needed, from food and drink, cleaning materials and fittings, to stationery and laundry, are delivered at the rear.

Parking lots

Car parking spaces are provided for employees, delivery services and visitors. The entrance and the exit to the garage are guarded by security.

Transportation

A network of bus and train routes or an underground train system carries people to and from their place of work.

Finance

People, businesses and governments all need money. Where does it come from? Usually, it is borrowed from someone who has money. As far as governments are concerned, that means you and me. They sell government stock which we buy with our savings. The government pays us back the money, plus a little bit more which is called interest. A business gets money by borrowing it from a bank or by selling its shares to individuals and companies on the stock market. The financial control of companies is handled by accountants; specialists or accountancy firms also provide specialist financial services to companies and individuals alike, including the statutory auditing (or checking) of company accounts. Insurance is another important financial services industry.

Computers dominate a stock exchange.

Activity in a large insurance office

Credit

Few people have enough money simply to buy the house of their choice. For example, when a couple get married and need a house to live in, how do they pay for it? They borrow the money they need from a credit corporation or savings and loan association. Then, over the next 25 years, they pay back the money, plus interest.

To buy a car, the money needed is borrowed, usually from a bank, and paid back with interest. To make buying easier, big stores issue credit cards. This type of smaller purchase and credit is now done without cash or writing a check. Some of the cards issued by banks and credit corporations debit their owners' accounts directly. This is done electronically and is exactly equivalent to a cash transaction. Banks supply credit or cash cards to use in nearly any country in place of money.

Similar cards, called smart cards, can contain complete information about a customer's bank account on a magnetic strip, and also contain a microprocessor to handle the transaction correctly.

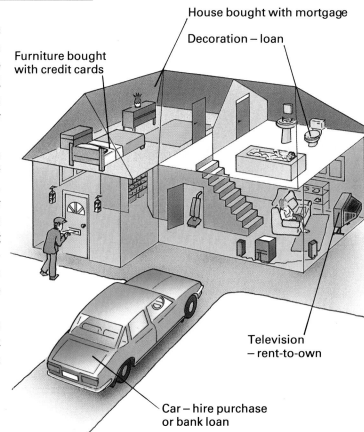
House bought with mortgage
Decoration – loan
Furniture bought with credit cards
Television – rent-to-own
Car – hire purchase or bank loan

Law

Laws of the kind we recognize today, enforceable rules and regulations, probably did not exist before ancient city-states, ruled by kings. These kings were called givers of laws. Today, governments are the modern law-givers, and lawyers form part of a large and important service industry. Lawyers have to interpret the law as it applies to businesses and individual people. But a large part of the law is based on past cases. Such case-histories are available on international computerized data bases. This helps lawyers resolve commercial disputes involving companies that operate in several countries.

When people break the law, society needs the services of a police force to find law-breakers and bring them to trial. People accused of crimes are tried in a court of law, where they are represented by lawyers, and if found guilty they are fined or imprisoned. Police forces, court employees and prison staffs all work in the service industry.

A policeman giving evidence in court

Food services

Food is produced on farms and plantations by the industry we call agriculture. Much of it is processed and packed by the food industry before going on sale in shops and stores. Stores, from small fast-food outlets to large supermarkets, form part of the retail trade, one of the major service industries in modern society. Supermarkets buy food products more cheaply than small local stores, and usually sell them at lower prices.

Getting money from a cash dispenser

Suction machines sorting eggs

By his or her 18th birthday, the average American has watched about 7,000 hours or 300 days of television. This includes more than 350,000 commercials.

The largest permanent cinema screen measures 92 × 69 feet. It is in Jakarta, the capital of Indonesia.

People do all kinds of things in their free time. Some may watch sports, go to the theater or a cinema, or go out for a meal in a restaurant. Other people may choose to stay at home and watch television or listen to music. Still others like to travel, and many people go abroad for their vacations. Some stay nearer home and visit historic sites or theme parks. Sports, entertainment, hotels, restaurants and travel are part of the huge leisure industry. And all of these activities are big business. They employ millions of people throughout the world.

Vacation industry

Most trips by air are made by people on vacation. In addition to providing most of the passengers for airlines, the vacation industry involves many other large businesses, including advertising, travel agencies, hotels and restaurants. The facilities of all of these may be coordinated by a large travel company, which sells a complete package holiday.

On a package holiday, ideally everything the holiday-maker wants is close at hand. The airport is not far from the hotel. The hotel has sports facilities, restaurants and may have a child-minding service. About half the vacations now taken abroad are package deals. By operating on such a large scale, a package holiday, including hotel rooms and meals, may cost no more than the regular airline ticket there and back.

Booking a vacation at a travel agency

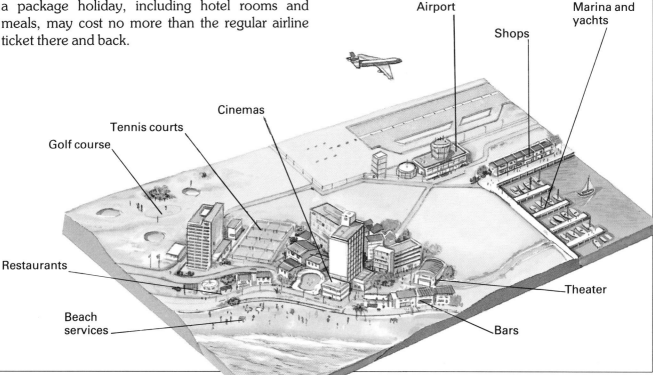

Airport

Shops

Marina and yachts

Cinemas

Tennis courts

Golf course

Restaurants

Beach services

Theater

Bars

TV and film

Cinema and television are the largest entertainment industries. In a little over 40 years, TV audiences have grown from a few thousand to more than 3 billion worldwide. Events of international interest, such as the Olympic Games, are viewed throughout the world. Studios and production companies have to work almost non-stop to keep the world's TV screens occupied. Many programs are exported, with the dialogue "dubbed" in another language or translated as subtitles. Some films, shown in the cinema or on TV, are also sold or hired as video recordings for people to watch in their own homes. Radio and music also provide home entertainment, and the international music industry produces millions of records, tapes and compact discs every year.

Film crew at work on location

Pleasure

An increasingly popular form of entertainment for the family is the theme park. Disneyland in Anaheim, California, pioneered some basic ideas. One of these is to recreate a historical episode, with moving, speaking mechanical figures, realistic background, and even smells. This has been taken further at EPCOT Center in Orlando, Florida. Here entertainment combined with instruction, animal exhibits and new ways of living are explored. Now these ideas have been exported to other countries. Elaborate fairgrounds, water parks and museums of industrial archaeology are varieties of theme parks.

Disneyland pioneered the theme park idea.

Sports

Because of television, international sports are now regularly viewed by millions. Hundreds of millions of people now see the Olympic Games as they take place. Golf and tennis have become spectator sports. Also because of television, minority sports that only a few followed, such as sumo wrestling, have become widely popular. American football and ice-hockey in Canada have achieved an international status because of satellite TV broadcasts. Large audiences attract advertisers. A successful professional player can earn more money from advertising than from playing.

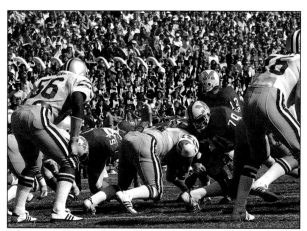
Many countries broadcast football.

There have been more discoveries in science and technology during the 20th century than in the whole of the rest of recorded history. Physicists have unravelled the secrets of the structure of the atom, making available a new source of power. And just as physicists have penetrated the atom, so have biologists revealed the secrets of the living cell, the key to which was the discovery of DNA and its structure.

Astronomers have aimed their radiotelescopes at the edge of the Universe, discovering pulsars and black holes. In aerospace, Frank Whittle's invention of the gas turbine – better known as the jet engine – revolutionized air transport. Rockets have landed on the Moon and sent probes to the outer planets.

The invention of radio, pioneered by Guglielmo Marconi, made possible worldwide communications. John Logie Baird was the first to send pictures by radio – he invented a type of television, which was later superseded by today's all-electronic system. Radar, another invention that uses radio frequencies, is now largely responsible for the safety of aircraft and ships.

Other 20th-century achievements include powered flight, the nuclear reactor, the computer, the transistor, the CAT scanner – the list is almost endless. During this century, humans have penetrated the ocean's deepest depths and have landed on the Moon. Nearly every achievement has involved the development of technology, applying various principles of science.

Nuclear power station, 1956

Nuclear power

The theory of relativity, described by Albert Einstein in 1905, is based on the idea that different observers, even when moving very fast, find that the laws of physics are identical. For example, the speed of light is the same however fast the person measuring it is moving. This theory led Einstein to propose that mass and energy are equivalent. When atoms of a heavy element, such as uranium, are split, the pieces weigh slightly less than the original atoms. This "missing" mass appears as energy, and is the source of energy in atom bombs and in nuclear reactors.

Frank Whittle, jet engine inventor

Holes in space

A black hole is the final stage in the life of a very large star. Such stars undergo a gravitational collapse. This means that all that remains of the star is packed very densely. The material at the center of a black hole can have many thousand million times the mass of our Sun, but may be only a few miles across. The gravitational field within a black hole is so strong that nothing, not even light, can escape from it. A large, spinning disc of matter forms around a black hole, and emits X rays (which is how astronomers find black holes). There are probably black holes in every galaxy. Some scientists think that the Universe will end when it becomes one big black hole.

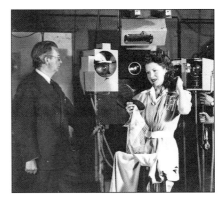

TV inventor John Baird

DNA

A living cell, whether it is part of you or a single bacterium, is a remarkable mechanism for producing complicated chemical substances. The discovery of the structure of DNA showed us how this works. Now scientists are able to genetically engineer DNA to, for example, make bacteria produce useful drugs.

GLOSSARY

Acid Chemical substance that, when dissolved in water, produces hydrogen ions.

Alkali chemical substance that neutralizes an acid.

Alloy mixture of two or more metals.

Ammonia strong, pungent-smelling alkali.

Antibiotic drug, usually from a bacterium (tiny living cell), that fights infection.

Atoms the tiny particles of which everything is made.

Barcode series of thick and thin lines identifying an item that can be read by a computer.

Biodegradable a substance is biodegradable if it soon rots.

Catalyst substance that speeds a chemical reaction without being used up.

Corrosion effect of exposure, such as rusting, on metals.

Electric arc powerful spark used to melt metals being welded, also an early form of lighting.

Fertilizer substance or substances added to soil to help plants grow.

Fuselage the body of an aircraft where the pilot and passengers sit.

Genetic engineering altering living cells to change how they work.

Information any kind of useful data.

Insulator material that does not conduct electricity; a material that prevents heat from passing.

Internal combustion engine usually a petrol or diesel engine where the combustion of fuel takes place inside the engine.

Kevlar remarkable plastic material used to make bullet-proof vests and strong cables.

Laminate layers of material sandwiched together to produce a stronger material.

Laser device that makes an intense beam of light of one precise color.

Microprocessor tiny electronic device carrying typically thousands of transistors – a computer on a chip.

Microwave oven oven that heats substances placed in it by causing their molecules to vibrate.

Molecule a group of atoms linked together.

Pacemaker device that controls irregular heartbeats with a minute regular electrical impulse.

Petrochemical a chemical that is made from petroleum or natural gas.

Pig iron crude iron, as it comes from a blast furnace.

Polymer a substance that contains very large molecules, each composed of small molecules linked together.

Polystyrene plastic foam for insulation or packing.

Polythene useful plastic for kitchen bowls and other containers.

Production line part of a factory where a series of operations to an object being made takes place one after the other.

PVC (polyvinyl chloride) useful plastic used to make records and tubing.

Reinforced concrete very strong concrete set around iron or steel bars.

Resin synthetic or natural substance that sets hard.

Satellite dish round dish that receives or sends satellite signals.

Shares units that represent the value of a company traded on a stock exchange.

Silicon chip a tiny piece of silicon, made from a special kind of sand, to which other materials are added to form a complete electrical circuit. Its development made possible the pocket-size calculators, radios, etc., that are available today.

Smelting melting metal ore in a furnace to extract pure metal.

Synthetic produced by chemical combinations, rather than of natural origin.

Titanium strong metal used in aircraft construction.

Transistor compact electronic device that controls the flow of electric current.

Vacuum tube large ancestor of transistor that also could control an electric current or switch it on and off.

INDEX

Photographic Credits:
Cover: Cinncinati Milacron; intro page and pages 5, 7 right, 9
left, 11, 18 bottom, 19 bottom and 33 top: J. Allan Cash; pages
6, 7 top, 9 bottom, 15 bottom, 19 left, 22, 30 left and right and
back cover: Zefa; pages 7 left, 9 right, 12, 15 top, 16, 20, 21, 26,
28, 31 right and 33 left and right: Robert Harding Library; pages
8 right, 18 top, left and right, 19 right, 24 and 31 left: Eye
Ubiquitous; page 31 top: Metropolitan Police; page 32: Network
Photographers.